Guitar Scales

JOE BENNETT

...To Go!

HAL•LEONARD®

Published by

Hal Leonard

Exclusive distributors:

Hal Leonard

7777 West Bluemound Road, Milwaukee, WI 53213

Email: info@halleonard.com

Hal Leonard Europe Limited

42 Wigmore Street Maryleborne, London, WIU 2 RN

Email: info@halleonardeurope.com

Hal Leonard Australia Pty. Ltd.

4 Lentara Court Cheltenham, Victoria, 9132 Australia

Email: info@halleonard.com.au

Order No. AM954261
ISBN 0-7119-7233-8

Written by Joe Bennett.
Book design and layout by Digital Music Art.
Cover design by Michael Bell Design.
Cover and text photographs by George
Taylor. Artist photographs courtesy of LFI.

Printed in EU.

www.halleonard.com

Guitar Scales To Go!

hatever style of music you play, whatever type of guitar you own, sooner or later you're going to want to 'play lead'. There are thousands of transcription books out there which feature solos by your favourite artists, with every bend, pull-off and pick-scrape lovingly reproduced, but what do you do when you want to make up your own solos and melodies?

You can, of course, go out and buy a scale book, but these really just function as a musical dictionary – they don't tell you how to apply the scales, or give advice on how your guitar solos are supposed to *sound* – which is what it's all about, right?

This book features over 40 of the most useful and exciting scales and positions that gigging and recording guitarists use. In addition, each scale includes a chord sheet – the idea is that once you've learned the scale, you can practise playing lead lines over the chords in order to hear how they sound in context. Remember, a scale only becomes worth listening to when *you* make a great solo out of it!

Diagrams explained

Fretboxes

Fretboxes show the guitar upright i.e. with the headstock, nut and tuning pegs at the top of the picture – six vertical lines represent the strings.

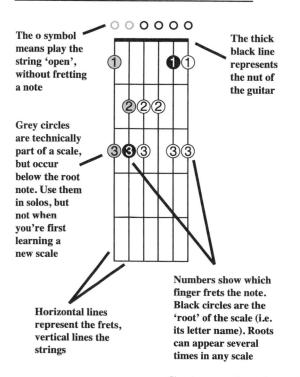

The o symbol means play the string 'open', without fretting a note

The thick black line represents the nut of the guitar

Grey circles are technically part of a scale, but occur below the root note. Use them in solos, but not when you're first learning a new scale

Horizontal lines represent the frets, vertical lines the strings

Numbers show which finger frets the note. Black circles are the 'root' of the scale (i.e. its letter name). Roots can appear several times in any scale

Notation and tablature

'Tab' is drawn with the guitar on its side, with the thickest string at the bottom – six horizontal lines represent the strings.

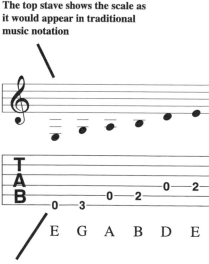

The top stave shows the scale as it would appear in traditional music notation

E   G   A   B   D   E

Below is the tablature – the numbers represent the fret positions. A zero means the string should be played open. The letters underneath the tab are the actual note names you're playing.

Many guitarists think they 'know' scales, sitting down and diligently learning all seven modes, for example, only to fall back on a couple of easy blues licks as soon as they play live.

Think of a scale as a set of notes which can be used to play a melody. That means that your lead part can contain any note from that scale, but it doesn't have to contain all of them, and they can be in any order.

When you practise a new scale, try to visualise it as a shape rather than as a long string of notes – this will help you to avoid playing boring, rambly solos, and allow you to improvise freely.

The most important technique is to pick the right scale in the first place. Generally, major-type scales (e.g. major, major pentatonic, 'country') sound better in major keys, and minor-type scales (e.g. minor, harmonic minor, minor pentatonic) sound better in minor keys. This simple rule works most of the time, but if it doesn't – experiment!

Finally, teach your ear as well as your fingers. Your aim is to be so familiar with a scale that you know how the lead line is going to sound *before* you play it. That way, you're playing the music that's in your head – this is true improvisation.

Practising

- All the scales in this book are shown ascending only. When you practise a scale, it should be played ascending and descending, without repeating the highest note.

- Play the scales evenly, so that each note is the same length. Don't speed up for easy sections and slow down for the more difficult bits. Use a metronome or drum machine, and fluency will develop naturally over time as you gradually increase the speed.

- Don't use any effects when you're learning a new scale. Distortion, overdrive and delay can fool you into thinking that you're playing better than you really are!

- Chord sheets are supplied throughout the book, each featuring chords which will sound good played as a backing for that particular scale. Record the sequence over and over again on tape, or get a friend to play the chords while you take a solo.

- Practise one scale at a time until it falls under your fingers comfortably.

Chord sheet – typical example

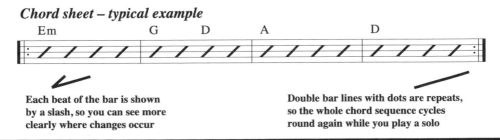

Each beat of the bar is shown by a slash, so you can see more clearly where changes occur

Double bar lines with dots are repeats, so the whole chord sequence cycles round again while you play a solo

Any scale can be played in one of the 12 musical keys – it's simply a question of moving your hand to the right fret position, and finding the scale's root note on one of the diagrams below. Root notes (shown in black circles in the fretboxes) give a scale its letter name. Apart from the 'easy scales' chapter, all other scales in the book are shown in the key of A, but they can be easily transposed to any of the other 11 keys. So it's worth remembering that once you can play a new shape, you've in fact learned 12 scales!

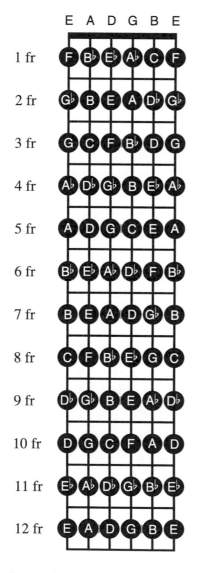

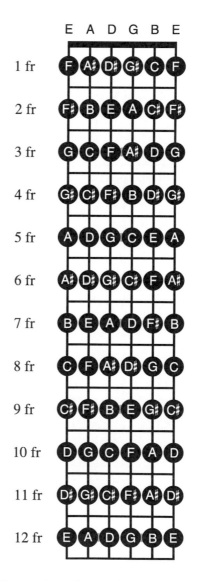

This diagram shows how to find any scale's root note, and will help you if the scale you want has a flat (♭) in its name.

This diagram shows the same information, but using alternate names for the notes. It will help you if the scale you want has a sharp (♯) in its name.

1

Easy Scales

As with chords, the first scales most people learn are in an 'open position', meaning they feature strings that aren't fretted. The advantage of these shapes is that they're easier to learn and can usually be played at greater speed. However, the open notes mean they can only be played in the keys shown, and some techniques (especially bends) are difficult in lower neck positions. Even so, the three scales shown in this section have been used by the likes of John Lee Hooker, Jimmy Page, John Squire and Noel Gallagher, so you're soloing in good company!

Em pentatonic

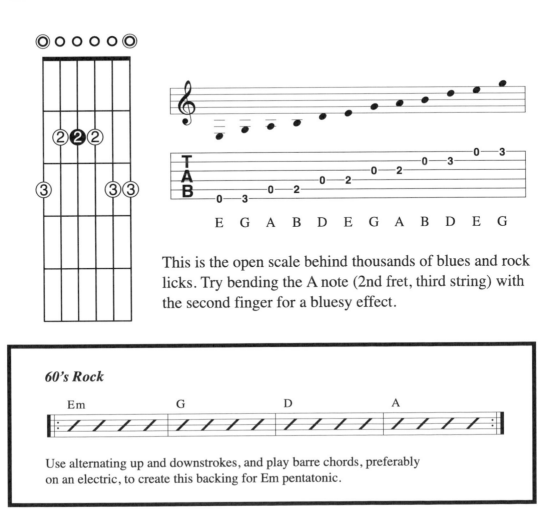

E G A B D E G A B D E G

This is the open scale behind thousands of blues and rock licks. Try bending the A note (2nd fret, third string) with the second finger for a bluesy effect.

60's Rock

Em   G   D   A

Use alternating up and downstrokes, and play barre chords, preferably on an electric, to create this backing for Em pentatonic.

G major pentatonic

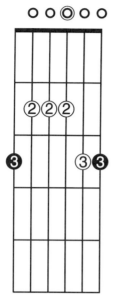

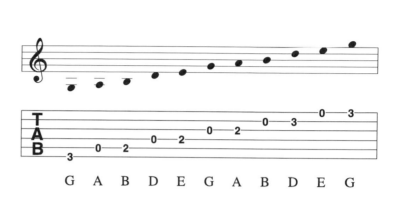

G A B D E G A B D E G

Major pentatonics have an upbeat, bright sound, and work well in country music, but you'll also hear them in folk, rock and jazz recordings.

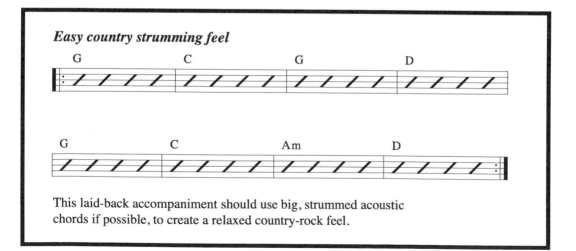

Easy country strumming feel

This laid-back accompaniment should use big, strummed acoustic chords if possible, to create a relaxed country-rock feel.

E blues

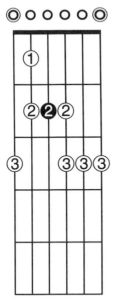

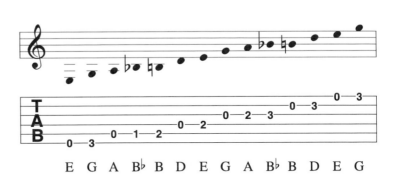

E G A B♭ B D E G A B♭ B D E G

The open E blues shape works over, er, blues in E!
Try not to linger on the B♭ notes too long because they
may clash with the backing chords at times during a solo.

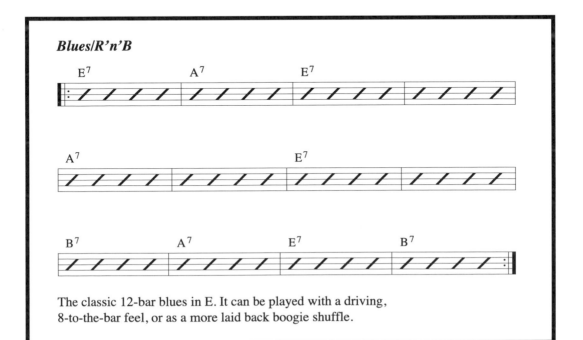

Blues/R'n'B

The classic 12-bar blues in E. It can be played with a driving,
8-to-the-bar feel, or as a more laid back boogie shuffle.

John Lee Hooker has been using the E blues scale for over 60 years!

2

Pentatonics

The pentatonic scale has long been a favourite with guitarists. It's got it all – not difficult to learn, uncomplicated fingering, and sounds OK whatever you play! The vast majority of beginners never venture outside position 1 of the minor pentatonic (below) because it's the easiest, but as you can see there are lots of other shapes on the fingerboard.

The name means that there are five notes in the octave, and these represent the five notes that the human ear finds most pleasing, which is why it doesn't matter so much which notes you play.

You'll find the minor pentatonic scale in particular is great for making up rock riffs.

Just because pentatonics are fairly simple, don't think that professional players never use them. Clapton's *Layla* riff uses the D minor pentatonic scale. David Gilmour's epic solo in Pink Floyd's *Comfortably Numb* features runs taken from B minor pentatonic. More contemporary British artists have continued the tradition – Oasis, The Stone Roses and Kula Shaker have all used major and minor pentatonics.

Am pentatonic

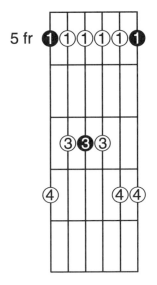

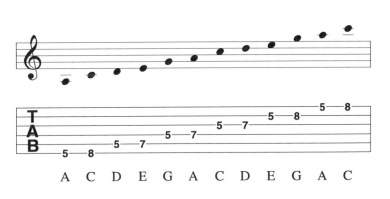

A C D E G A C D E G A C

This well-used but still hugely versatile box shape is the saviour of many a rock soloist. Try using hammer-ons and pull-offs between fretted notes.

Am pentatonic

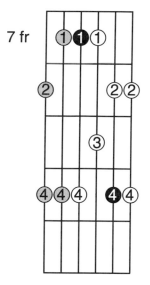

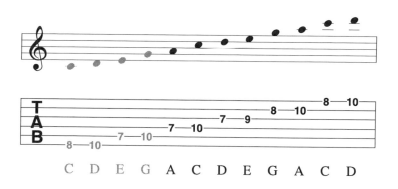

C   D   E   G   A   C   D   E   G   A   C   D

Position 2 is a little more awkward, but it does have the advantage of moving further up the neck, which may present you with new improvising ideas.

Am pentatonic

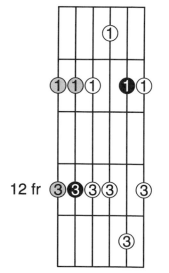

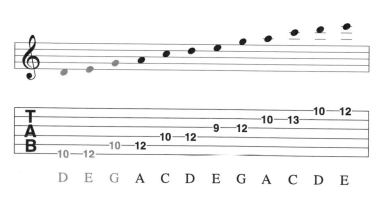

D   E   G   A   C   D   E   G   A   C   D   E

Because of its two position shifts, few players use this shape in its entirety, but small fragments of it can be useful as you move to another position.

Am pentatonic

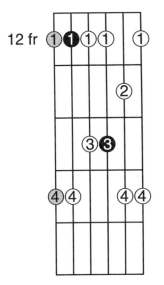

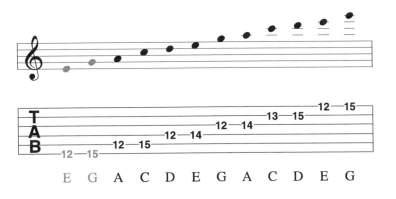

E G A C D E G A C D E G

This shape is often favoured by blues players such as Gary Moore or B.B. King. Any note played with the little finger can be bent up a whole tone (2 frets' worth).

Am pentatonic

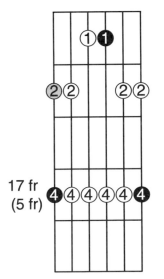

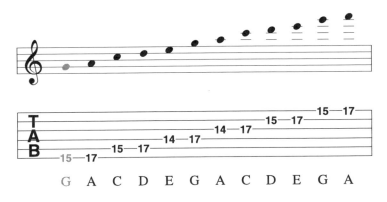

G A C D E G A C D E G A

This high-altitude shape is perfect for squealy blues-rock moments too. Don't try the 17th fret position on an acoustic unless you're very brave – or very strong!

Guitar Scales To Go!

Minor Blues

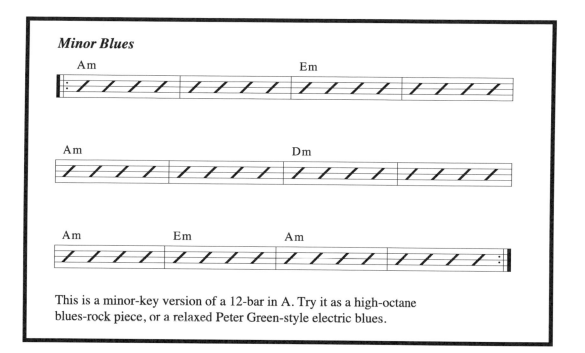

This is a minor-key version of a 12-bar in A. Try it as a high-octane blues-rock piece, or a relaxed Peter Green-style electric blues.

Mid-tempo British Rock

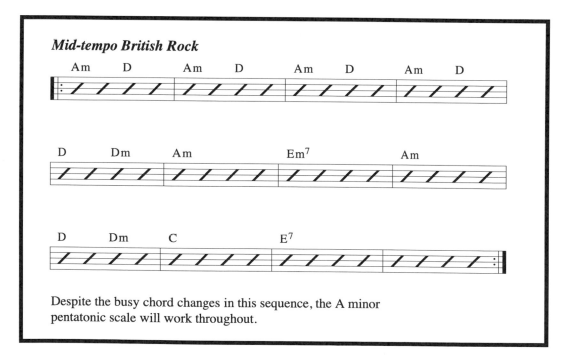

Despite the busy chord changes in this sequence, the A minor pentatonic scale will work throughout.

A major pentatonic

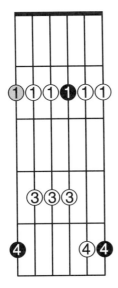

F♯ A B C♯ E F♯ A B C♯ E F♯ A

Although this looks very like the basic A minor pentatonic shape, note that it's played three frets lower, so the root note is played with the fourth finger.

A major pentatonic

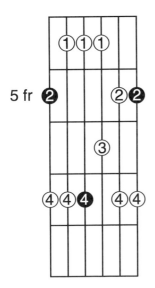

A B C♯ E F♯ A B C♯ E F♯ A B

This is a simplified version of the traditional major scale shape shown on page 22 – it just misses some notes out. Note that the root note is played with the second finger.

A major pentatonic

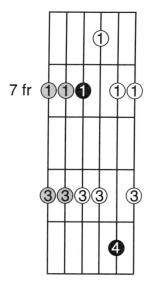

7 fr

B C♯ E F♯ A B C♯ E F♯ A B C♯

Despite some awkward position shifts, this pattern is well worth learning for the great hammer-ons and pull-offs you can do on the first two strings.

A major pentatonic

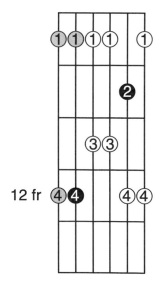

12 fr

C♯ E F♯ A B C♯ E F♯ A B C♯ E

This shape gets the second finger working, so you don't rely too much on the stronger first and third. Again, try pull-offs and hammer-ons at the top of the scale.

A major pentatonic

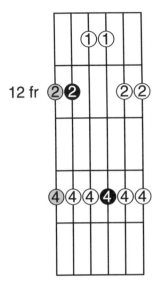

E F♯ A B C♯ E F♯ A B C♯ E F♯

This one might appear a little strange at first, but it's easier than it looks – just use one finger per fret throughout and the fingering should fall into place.

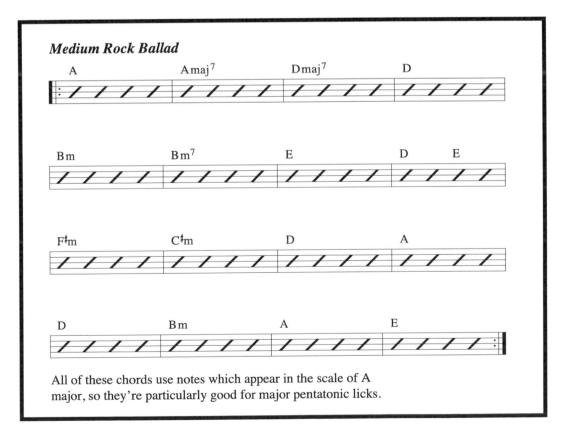

Medium Rock Ballad

All of these chords use notes which appear in the scale of A major, so they're particularly good for major pentatonic licks.

Hendrix was mainly a minor pentatonic man, but also used major pentatonics and blues scale shapes in his solos.

A blues

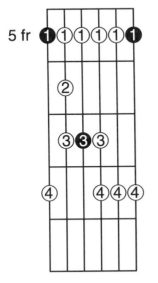

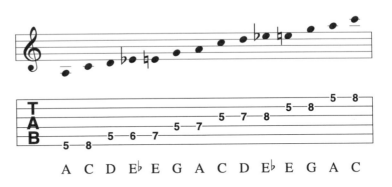

A   C   D   E♭   E   G   A   C   D   E♭   E   G   A   C

Although the blues scale isn't strictly a pentatonic shape, it's included here because it's really a minor pentatonic box shape with a passing note added (the E♭ shown here).

A blues

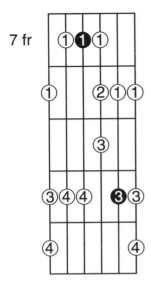

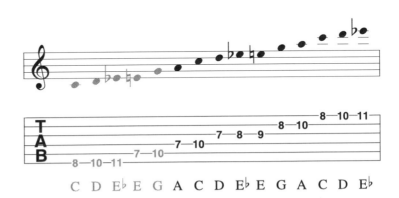

C   D   E♭   E   G   A   C   D   E♭   E   G   A   C   D   E♭

Because this is the most difficult of the blues scale box shapes to play, you may find it easier if some notes are played by sliding into position. Sounds good, too!

A blues

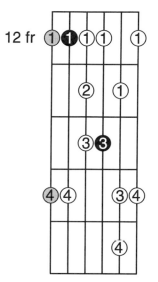

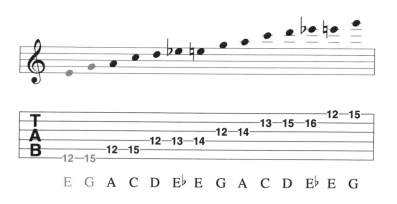

E G A C D E♭ E G A C D E♭ E G

This is the full version of the scale in this position, but many guitarists prefer to play it without the position shift by omitting the little finger note on the second string.

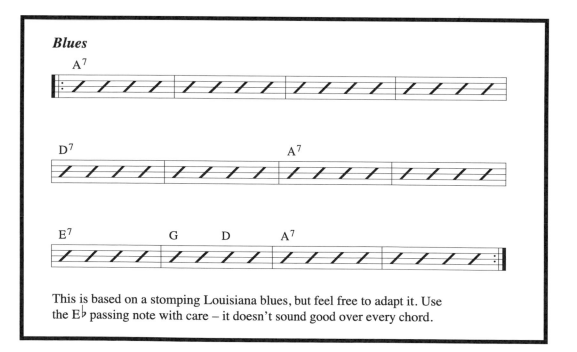

Blues

This is based on a stomping Louisiana blues, but feel free to adapt it. Use the E♭ passing note with care – it doesn't sound good over every chord.

A country

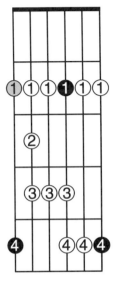

F# A B C C# E F# A B C C# E F# A

If the blues scale is a minor pentatonic with a passing note, this is the major pentatonic's equivalent. Practise the ascending scale with hammer-ons – you'll need them!

A country

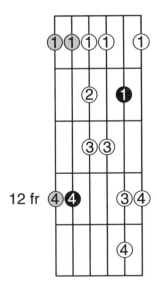

C# E F# A B C C# E F# A B C C# E

The middle part of this scale shape is the most useful in an up-tempo solo, because it can be played at fairly high speed without a position shift.

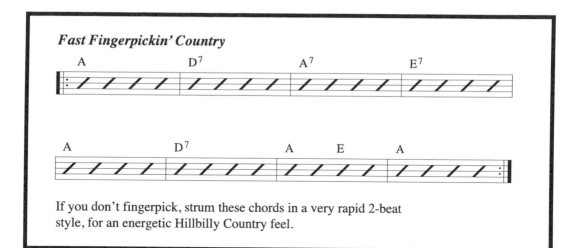

Fast Fingerpickin' Country

If you don't fingerpick, strum these chords in a very rapid 2-beat style, for an energetic Hillbilly Country feel.

When Chet Atkins ain't fingerpickin', he likes nothin' better than a barn-stompin' country scale solo line.

3

Major Scales

All of Western music – indeed, most of the world's music – owes something to the major scale. It provides the background for all musical harmony and theory. So it's perhaps surprising that guitarists don't use it more often.

The reason for this is that major scales sound very melodic and 'nice' – too nice, in fact, for aggressive genres like rock, metal and funk. But even if you are exclusively a rock player, it's still worth learning all five major scale fingerboard positions. As you learn new scales, patterns will begin to emerge which make reference to the major scale, and all of the modes have intervals and fingerboard shapes which are lifted from a major box shape. The major scale itself is also known as the 'Ionian mode' (see page 30).

If you use the major scale for soloing over chord changes, avoid playing too 'scalically'. It's all too easy to play six or seven notes from the scale in a row, and turn your epic solo into something that sounds like a piano student practising for their exams. But don't give up – major scale solos will put you in the company of George Benson, Hank Marvin, Nuno Bettencourt and George Harrison.

A major

This convenient shape covers more than two whole octaves – slide it up to the 15th fret and you can double that range. Essential study!

A major

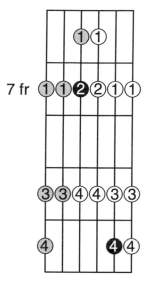

B C♯ D E F♯ G♯ A B C♯ D E F♯ G♯ A B C♯ D

Although lots of these notes are greyed-out (i.e. they're lower than the lowest root note) do explore this region of the shape – it's almost a whole octave.

A major

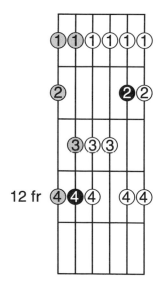

C♯ D E F♯ G♯ A B C♯ D E F♯ G♯ A B C♯ D E

You might like to think of this shape as being based on an open C chord fingering – the notes can also form the finger shapes for open chords of F, Am, Dm, and G.

A major

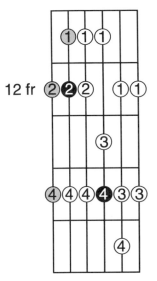

12 fr

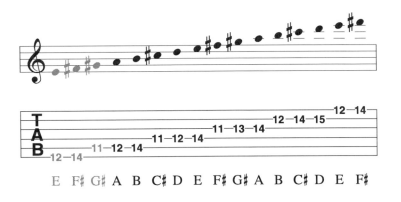

E F♯ G♯ A B C♯ D E F♯ G♯ A B C♯ D E F♯

Another position shift, but not a particularly difficult one. There are some opportunities to play double-stops (i.e. two notes on adjacent strings) if you re-finger this shape.

A major

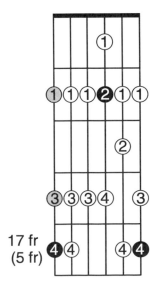

17 fr
(5 fr)

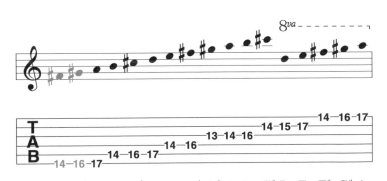

F♯ G♯ A B C♯ D E F♯ G♯ A B C♯ D E F♯ G♯ A

Like most of the shapes, this A major scale works in the position shown, and also 12 frets lower. This one's good for rapid playing on the first two strings.

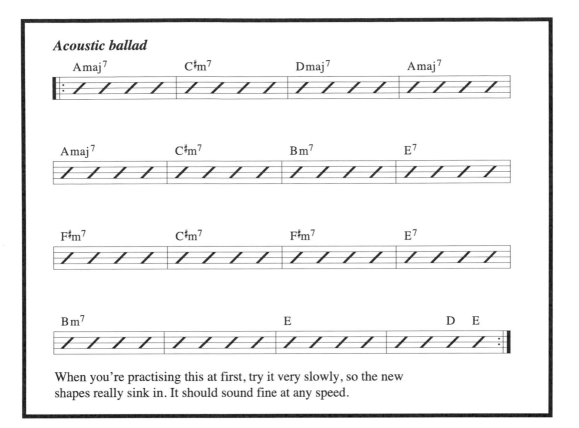

Acoustic ballad

| Amaj^7 | C$\sharp$m^7 | Dmaj^7 | Amaj^7 |
| / / / / | / / / / | / / / / | / / / / |

| Amaj^7 | C$\sharp$m^7 | Bm^7 | E^7 |
| / / / / | / / / / | / / / / | / / / / |

| F$\sharp$m^7 | C$\sharp$m^7 | F$\sharp$m^7 | E^7 |
| / / / / | / / / / | / / / / | / / / / |

| Bm^7 | | E | D   E |
| / / / / | / / / / | / / / / | / / / / |

When you're practising this at first, try it very slowly, so the new shapes really sink in. It should sound fine at any speed.

The ever-smiling Hank Marvin, no doubt contemplating yet another major key Shadows' melody.

4

Minor Scales

If you find that minor pentatonic solos have suited you thus far, you really should check out the minor scale. It contains all of the notes of the minor pentatonic, plus a couple more that can be used to expand the melodic possibilities of your lead lines.

As with the major scale, it's shown here in five positions (and remember that many of these can be played an octave higher simply by moving them up 12 frets). Don't feel that you need to follow every position shift exactly as shown here – in many cases, you'll be able to come up with good

ideas simply by using part of one minor position.

Minor scales really only work in minor keys. Major chords may occur within a minor sequence, but the overall feel will remain minor.

When guitarists talk about minor scales, they mean the 'natural minor', also known technically as the Aeolian mode. It's not to be confused with the equally well-known (but far less versatile) harmonic minor scale shown on page 38. Notable minor scale guitar players include Mark Knopfler and Carlos Santana.

A minor

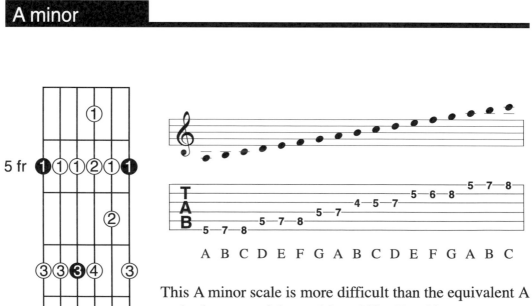

A B C D E F G A B C D E F G A B C

This A minor scale is more difficult than the equivalent A major because of the position shifts. For this reason, some players favour the 12th fret version (see over the page).

A minor

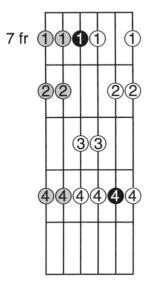

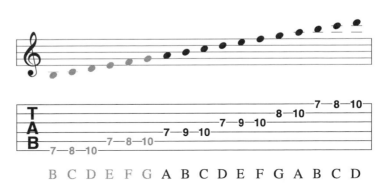

B C D E F G A B C D E F G A B C D

Minor scales work particularly well in this little-used position because you're using one finger per fret, which will enable you to develop speed much more easily.

A minor

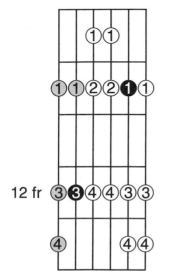

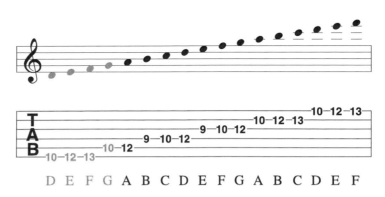

D E F G A B C D E F G A B C D E F

Playing the root with your third finger may feel strange, but it's worth practising so that you can play the lower greyed-out notes in a solo.

A minor

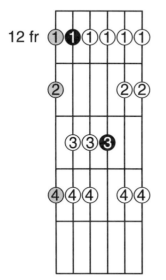

12 fr

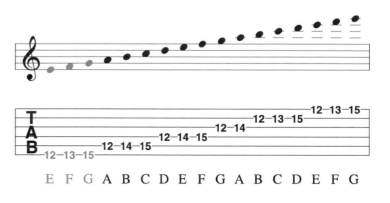

E F G A B C D E F G A B C D E F G

This is the easiest and perhaps the most versatile of the natural minor box shapes. Bend the top note up two frets' worth and you can get the high A.

A minor

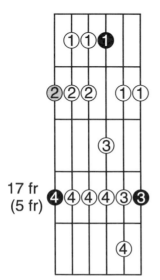

17 fr
(5 fr)

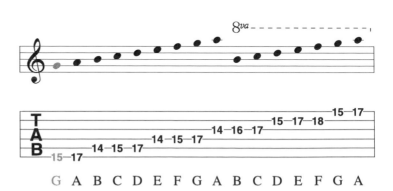

G A B C D E F G A B C D E F G A

Depending on which octave you choose for this position, you can get 1950's-style twang (5th fret) or mellow jazz-fusion tones (17th fret).

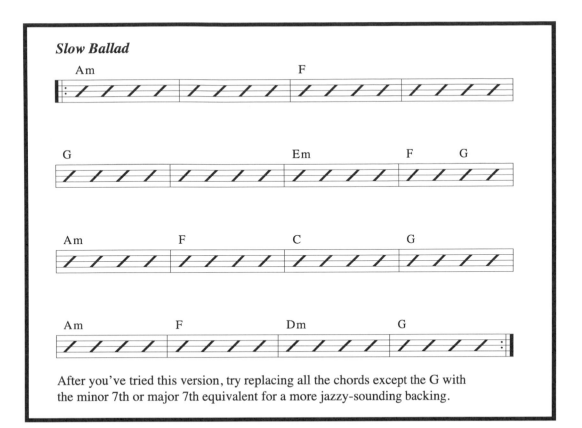

Slow Ballad

After you've tried this version, try replacing all the chords except the G with the minor 7th or major 7th equivalent for a more jazzy-sounding backing.

Mark Knopfler of Dire Straits – Minor for Nothin'.

5

Modes

Guitarists talk more rubbish about modes than they do about amp tone, and that's saying something! It's worth getting one thing straight right now – modes aren't any different from any other sort of scale. Like all scales, they all have a particular character, and like all scales, each mode is suited to specific chords or styles. The only reason they are in a category of their own is that they all come from the same (Ancient Greek) background, and so have appropriately exotic-sounding names. In rough order of importance for guitarists, these are;

Ionian, Aeolian, Mixolydian, Dorian, Lydian, Phrygian, and Locrian. As mentioned in previous chapters, the Ionan and Aeolian modes are just ordinary major and minor scales anyway, and it's best to think of the others as major or minor scales with a couple of notes altered.

In this chapter, you'll find all of the most useful fingerings for all but one of the modes. We've deliberately missed out the bizarre-sounding Locrian mode on the grounds that no guitarist has ever made a complete solo out of it. Well, not one that you'd like.

A Mixolydian

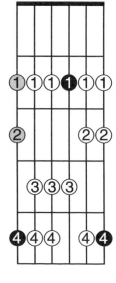

F♯ G A B C♯ D E F♯ G A B C♯ D E F♯ G A

The Mixolydian mode works particularly well in R & B styles, although it can sound 'Eastern' too (e.g. Led Zeppelin). It's just a major scale with a flattened 7th.

Crispian Mills, of Hindie-rockers Kula Shaker. Their debut album 'K' has the Mixolydian mode all over it.

A Mixolydian

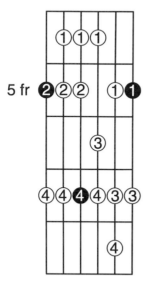

A B C♯ D E F♯ G A B C♯ D E F♯ G A B

This position demonstrates the Mixolydian mode's similarity to the major scale. Compare it to the shape shown on page 22 – only the 7th note is different.

Medium Funk

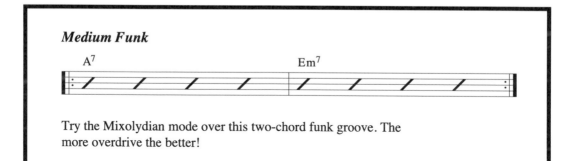

Try the Mixolydian mode over this two-chord funk groove. The more overdrive the better!

MODAL MYTHS

Guitar-shop-speak translated

"The Dorian's the second mode, so play it over D minor"

This may be true, but can be confusing if you're trying to learn what modes are all about. Like any scale, modes can be played from any root note. The Dorian is indeed a minor mode, but over a chord of Dm you could equally play a D minor scale, or D pentatonic minor, or D blues, for example, depending on the sound you want. The Dorian is a minor scale with one note altered – that's all.

"Play G Dorian, then C Mixolydian, then F Ionian"

The whole idea of modal harmony and melody is that you stay in the same mode – you don't keep skipping shapes every time there's a chord change. Modes can be thought of as musical keys in their own right, with their own chord sets and scales. Check out the chord sheets throughout this chapter to see examples of modal harmony patterns in a musical context.

A Dorian

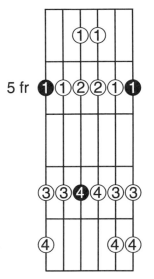

A B C D E F♯ G A B C D E F♯ G A B C

The Dorian mode – or, if you prefer, a normal minor scale with the 6th note raised. We've shown three shapes for this extremely useful mode.

A Dorian

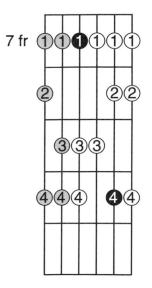

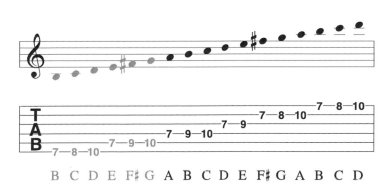

B C D E F♯ G A B C D E F♯ G A B C D

This fingering-friendly box shape is often used in the rhythmic solos of the legendary Carlos Santana. The top note can be bent up two frets' worth.

A Dorian

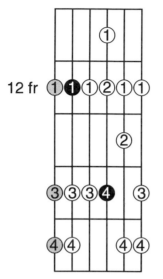

12 fr

E F#G A B C D E F#G A B C D E F#G

If you don't like the position shift involved in this slightly more difficult shape, just re-finger the notes and play the top seven notes of the scale.

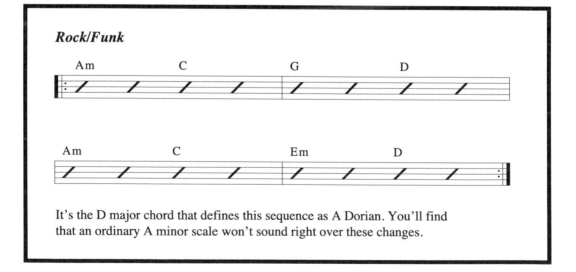

Rock/Funk

Am   C   G   D

Am   C   Em   D

It's the D major chord that defines this sequence as A Dorian. You'll find that an ordinary A minor scale won't sound right over these changes.

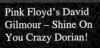
Pink Floyd's David
Gilmour – Shine On
You Crazy Dorian!

A Lydian

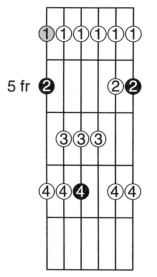

G# A B C# D# E F# G# A B C# D# E F# G# A B

Think of the Lydian mode as a major scale with the fourth note raised by one fret – again, compare it to the major box shape on page 22.

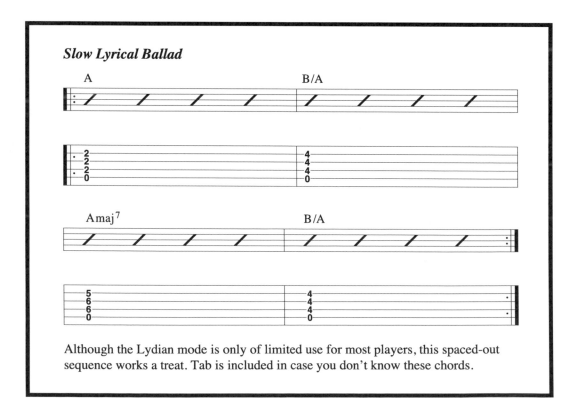

Although the Lydian mode is only of limited use for most players, this spaced-out sequence works a treat. Tab is included in case you don't know these chords.

A Phrygian

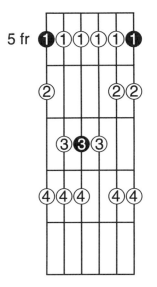

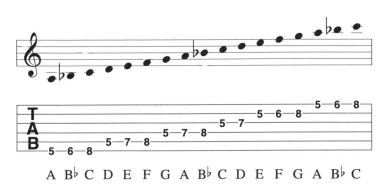

A B♭ C D E F G A B♭ C D E F G A B♭ C

Minor scale with a flattened second, but to you and me, it's that flamenco-sounding scale. It's almost impossible to apply this scale in rock and pop.

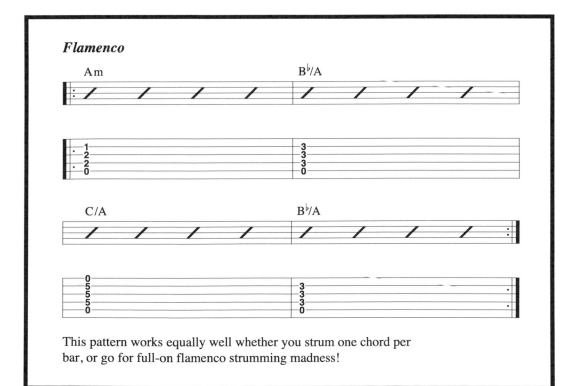

Flamenco

This pattern works equally well whether you strum one chord per bar, or go for full-on flamenco strumming madness!

6

Weird And Wonderful!

This chapter features a mishmash of some of the more unusual scales, used mainly by jazzers, and occasionally by rock players looking to spice up their solos. Some of them are not to be used throughout a solo – for example, the harmonic minor scale's main function in guitar solos is to play over the 'five chord' – in the key of A minor, this would be a chord of E or E7. The melodic 'jazz' minor and 'altered' scale are also included as an introduction to jazz soloing.

A harmonic minor

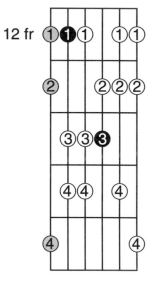

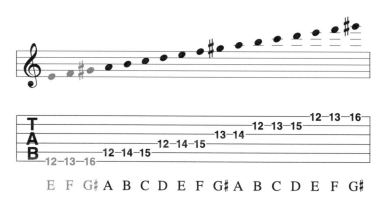

E F G♯ A B C D E F G♯ A B C D E F G♯

…also known as a minor scale with a raised 7th. If there's a chord change in a minor key sequence where the normal minor scale doesn't sound right, try this.

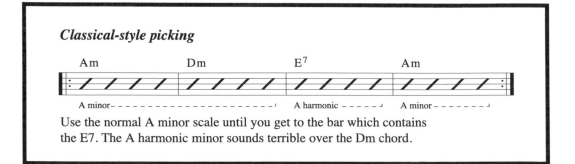

Classical-style picking

| Am | Dm | E7 | Am |

A minor –' A harmonic – – – – – ⌐ A minor – – – – – – – ⌐

Use the normal A minor scale until you get to the bar which contains the E7. The A harmonic minor sounds terrible over the Dm chord.

A melodic minor

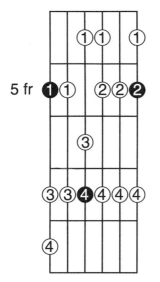

A B C D E F♯ G♯ A B C D E F♯ G♯ A B

If you take a major scale and make it minor just by flattening the third note, you get this curious beast. It instantly makes any minor solo sound 'jazzy'.

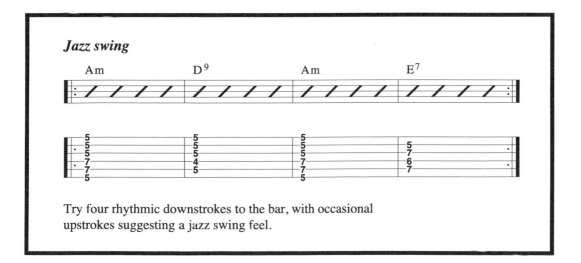

Try four rhythmic downstrokes to the bar, with occasional upstrokes suggesting a jazz swing feel.

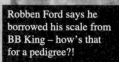
Robben Ford says he borrowed his scale from BB King – how's that for a pedigree?!

A minor pentatonic major 6th

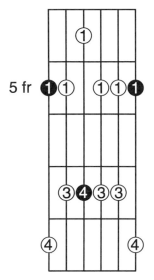

5 fr

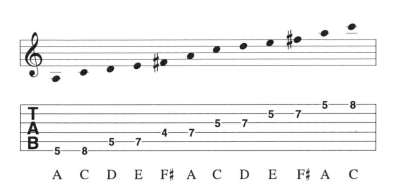

A C D E F♯ A C D E F♯ A C

This is often called the 'Robben Ford scale' after the blues player that popularised it. It's an interesting alternative to straightforward minor pentatonics.

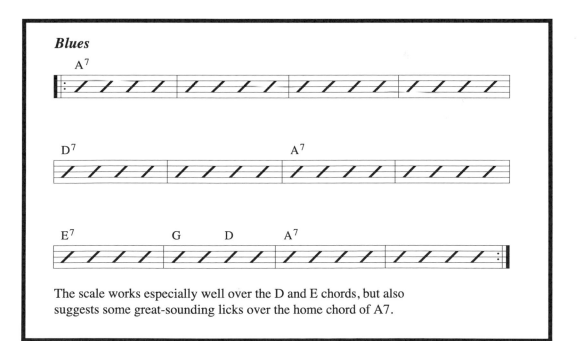

Blues

A⁷

D⁷   A⁷

E⁷   G   D   A⁷

The scale works especially well over the D and E chords, but also suggests some great-sounding licks over the home chord of A7.

A altered

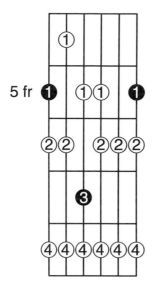

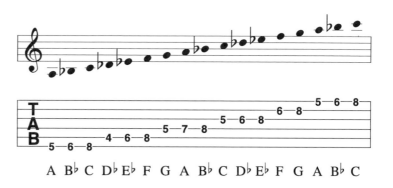

A B♭ C D♭ E♭ F G A B♭ C D♭ E♭ F G A B♭ C

Just like the harmonic minor and diminished scales, this jazz favourite is mainly used over 'five' chords. Use it elsewhere at your own risk!

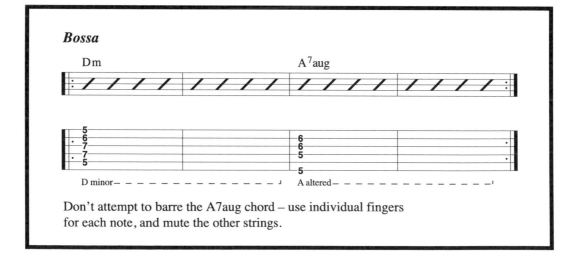

Bossa

Don't attempt to barre the A7aug chord – use individual fingers for each note, and mute the other strings.

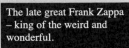

A whole tone

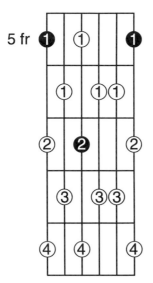

5 fr

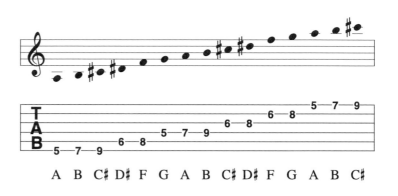

A B C♯ D♯ F G A B C♯ D♯ F G A B C♯

The whole tone scale means just that – i.e. the space between each note is two frets' worth. It's most effective when played over augmented chords.

Bossa

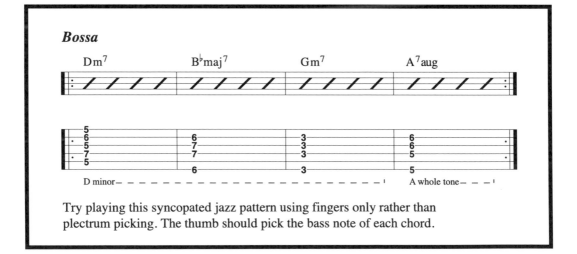

Dm⁷   B♭maj⁷   Gm⁷   A⁷aug

D minor— — — — — — — — — — — — — — — — — — — ＇   A whole tone— — —＇

Try playing this syncopated jazz pattern using fingers only rather than plectrum picking. The thumb should pick the bass note of each chord.

A diminished

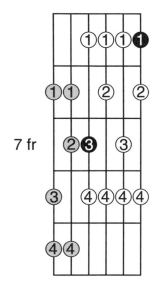

7 fr

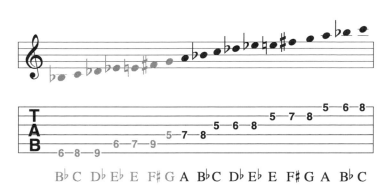

B♭ C D♭ E♭ E F♯ G A B♭ C D♭ E♭ E F♯ G A B♭ C

Although you *can* use these scales over the relevant diminished chord, they're more common over the 'five' chord – e.g. in a D major sequence, this would be A7.

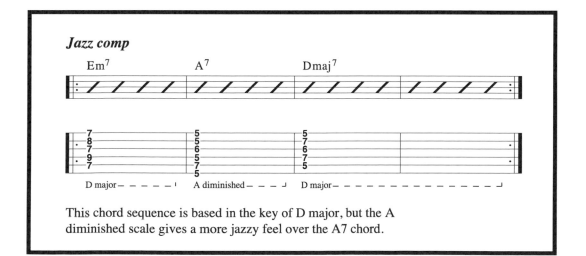

Jazz comp

This chord sequence is based in the key of D major, but the A diminished scale gives a more jazzy feel over the A7 chord.

Jazzer Pat Metheny
knows his diminished
from his whole tone.

Learning a new scale isn't the same as learning a new chord – you can't just go and use it straight away. It takes time to get used to its character, and to train your ear to recognise which of the notes work over certain chords. But learning a new scale, or even just a new position for a scale you already know, is a great way of getting your lead playing out of the musical ruts we all find ourselves in from time to time.

On this final page, I've supplied some hints and tips on how to turn your hard-learned scales into meaningful solos and riffs. But whatever you want to do with scales, keep this in mind; when I'm teaching electric guitar players, the most common mistake they make is to play scales far too fast, without really listening to the result. If your ear develops half as fast as your dexterity, you'll be well on the road to being a truly great musician.

Do...

- ...use phrasing. This means playing in musical 'sentences', so the solo can pause at the end of one phrase before it starts the next. Good phrasing gives the listener an opportunity to digest what they've just heard. Remember, the chord backing will carry on while your barrage of notes takes a breather.

- ...experiment with timing. Try playing a quick run of four or five short notes, followed by a couple of long, slow ones.

- ...use techniques. You can slide up to, or down to, any note of a scale. Try hammer-ons, pull-offs and vibrato to add interest.

- ...think like a singer. Once you've played a scale, sing a short musical phrase to yourself, and see if you can figure it out on the guitar.

- ...train your ear. Try singing a scale to yourself, then check by playing it back on the guitar to see how familiar you are with its character.

- ...play intervals. Why should your solo always go from one note in a scale to the next? Skip a few notes now and again.

- ...show off! If you find that a particular pattern of taps, hammer-ons or pull-offs helps you to play a scale pattern more rapidly, go for it!

- ...play round the chords. If one note of a scale doesn't sound right over the current chord, try another note from the same scale.

- ...emphasise notes that work well. If a note sounds great over any chord, keep coming back to it every time the chord appears again.

Don't...

- ...ramble. If you just play up and down the scale at random while the chords cycle past, the audience won't get an idea that there's an interesting guitar melody going on. As a general rule, if you've been playing for more than 4 bars without any rests or long notes, it's time to relax for a couple of beats.

- ...necessarily start solos on the root note. Just because you're playing in F#, say, it doesn't mean that the lead part has to begin on that note.

- ...over-use bends. Only a few notes of any scale will sound right when bent. Experiment to find out which these are for each new scale.

- ...use too many effects. The point of learning a new scale is to supply new melodic ideas, so don't blur these with loads of delay and fuzz.

- ...rely too much on 'licks'. These are previously-learned phrases that are played from memory. This will ultimately limit your solos.

- ...play 'scalically' all the time. Running up and down the scale, even at high speed, doesn't always create the most musical result.

- ...try to play too fast. Make sure every note of the scale sounds out cleanly and clearly at a slow tempo before you attempt anything flash.

- ...ignore the chords. If you don't think a note works over a chord, go back and check. Then you won't make the same mistake again.

- ...worry about breaking the rules. If you find a scale that doesn't appear in this book, but you like the way it sounds, use it!